Mahogany Musings

Poems For The People • Volume III

LOVE AND LOSS

TERESIA SIMMONS

Mahogany Musings Book Series, Poems for the People Volume III,
Love and Loss

Published in the United States, Aiseret Publishing.
Teresia.Simmons@gmail.com

First Edition
ISBN: 979-8-9859966-2-3

Dedication

To all those who have experienced Eros, Philos or Agape Love... and to all who have lost the feelings, ties or persons... all I can say is, we've made it. Let's cherish the moments and the memories.

Contents

My Life's Journey

I am bombarded with thoughts feelings,
Longings and desires.
What road am I taking now,
At this stage of my life?
Am I observing?
Am I learning?
Am I taking advantage of this time?
Am I really living?
My eyes and senses are open to new possibilities.
I am bombarded with thoughts,
Feelings and sensations.
Oh, my life's journey.

A Celebration Of You

A celebration of you
I said good bye to
My friend, lover and my confidant
My personal coach and cheerleader
You gave me a chance to reach inside myself and
See all of my potentiality
If I had fears or doubts
You always encouraged
If I was hesitant or unsure
You encouraged
You lived your life to the fullest, without reserve.
You had a passion for your
Children, coaching, friends and for me
I am remembering
All the good times spent together
Your beautiful smile
Your big shouldered embraces
Your mischievous eyes and absolute sexiness
Your smooth chocolate skin
Your deep, throaty, earthy laugh
I am remembering your bangles jangling
And your passion for fashion
Oh, and you sure could dance
I am saying goodbye
Celebrating the memories

Of you and what you brought to my life
I love you and I always will
Goodbye my love
I'll see you again in another time and place
Celebrating you.

A Missed Life

Did you see that beautiful sunset?
That glorious display as autumn trees
Losing their coats of many colors?

Did you miss the radiant shades
Glimmering in the sky?
Or the beautiful sounds of the oceans
Lapping upon the shore?

Did you miss the beautiful memories of
Childhood innocence?
Perhaps those of the woman who once held you
As you suckled at her breast?

Did you miss the twinkle in your child's eyes?
Or the squeals of delight
From the basking of being present?

Did you miss the moment?
Miss the joy?
Miss out on life?
On love?

Now
Death is here, calling your name.
Did you miss the moment?
Miss your life?

Alone

When I'm alone
I think of you

And I dream of things
That could be
Should be
Or would be

Alone
I can feel my heart bursting with
Feelings of love and
Great pain

Alone
Recalling

Alone
Why?

Alone
Life is so short

Alone
With thoughts of you.

Amazing

It is so amazing that I met you
I was there and so were you
Our paths crossed
And now our lives have become one

Never once imagining that my life
Would touch yours

It's amazing and it's a blessing to
Have had this chance for this moment
And for you.

A Woman's Heart

If a man could just understand that
A woman needs to feel like she is his Queen
That she is loved, deserved and needed,
Then anything is possible.

When a woman feels that
She is the sexiest thing on earth
That she can make her man's heart
Quiver with joy, then anything is possible.

If a man really looks into the heart of this Woman
He will find
Love
Caring
Commitment
Joy
And a dear friend.

If a man can just understand that
He only has to look
To the woman standing
By his side for elation and bliss.

If a man can just understand this fact
He will have all the joy his heart can hold.

Black Woman

I am a woman of the darker hue
My rich supple body has borne
The seeds of greatness
My arms and breasts have nurtured
Kings and Presidents
My ready smile and steadfastness have
Rescued my young and cared for the old
I am tall and small
Bony and full-figured
I am hip, I am reserved
I am brave
I am what is needed to provide sanctity
Amidst the savagery of this world
I am wide-lipped and broad-nosed
I am throaty with a sexy voice
Raised in protest
And lulling in song
I am the old
I am the young
I am brave and strong
I am sensual
Sensuous
Sexy and demanding
I am weak and I am strong
I can be strident and militant
Fighting for my beliefs and
Fighting for my man

I am kind and compassionate
My hair is tight and close
Long and soft
I am a woman of many dimensions
I am the substance needed to keep myself
My man and my children free and
Safe from harm
I am the original earth mother providing for her
Young Standing by her man and
Willing to die
To protect them all

I am the Black Woman
I am a Queen to be
Loved
Respected
Adored
And
Admired throughout the entire world

Can't You See?

Do you really know how I feel?
Do you really care?
Can't you see?

Whatever I am dealing with
Will eventually be on your doorstep.

You cannot
Ignore
Rationalize or
Forget me.

Each of us is connected.
We are together
Forever linked in this
Chain of life.

Do you actually care?
Or is that a facade to mask
Your truth
Your myopic vision
Your past
Your feelings?

Hey!
Focus!
Stop!
Just Listen!

Let's let down our guards and
Just be
For real.

Curses to Dementia

Silence, shouting
Unsaid words reverberate in
My mind
My heart
My brain
I can't get through.

Still the Silence
Anger
Pain
Confusion
Lost memories
Permeate the room like a heavy stench of some
Long decayed or long dead beast.
I sit
I stand
I ask
I listen
I wait
Longing like a vapor of a discarded, spent cigarette.
How to bridge the silence?

Fear of loud sounds
Fear of loud shouts,
Disdainful expressions
Muddling
Tears.

Silence
Lack of understanding
No comprehension
An uncrossed bridge to discounted loneliness
I can't get through.

The
Silence is deafening.
Drowning
The relief of a few spoken words of love is what
I need.
Yet, the silence remains.
Curses to dementia.

Decision

It was my decision
But my heart still remembers

It was my decision
But I still care

It was my decision
But my stomach still does a flip flop

When I see you
My heart still remembers

It was my decision
But things don't change
And life goes on

It was my decision
It was not easy
Because my heart
Still remembers

Deer In Headlights

A deer in the headlights is my feeling this day
I am paralyzed in every muscle
In every vein
Unable to move from the pain
A deer in the headlights paralyzed by the
Danger of
Imminent pain
Seeing the pain coming in the bright glare
Coming into contact
Paralyzed by the bright, blinding
Searing light of approaching
Death and pain
A deer caught in the soaring
Blinding light of my emotional pain

Deja Vue!

Deja Vue?
This feels so familiar.
Been here before.

Deja Vue?
Or just plain romance?
Illusions or mere random wishes.
But this feels so familiar.
Been here before.
Deja Vue!

Desperation After Devastation

Right now I am so hurt and angry
How could you do this to me?
I feel betrayed and mistreated
How could you do this to me?
I feel betrayed and mistreated.
How could you, the one
I gave so much of my love and care
Leave me this way?
As your wife,
Didn't I deserve to be protected?
Provided for?
Covered by you?

Under the shadow of your care
Love is an action verb.
By your purposeful deeds
Your true intentions were shown.
Devastated
Demolished
Squished in the sadness of
Your acts
Your absence
Your neglect.

I am kneeling at Your feet, Lord.
You know what he did and didn't do
To and for me, his wife.
I am asking You to help me
Move from this place of
Hurt and betrayal.

He's gone. I'm still here.
Only You, Lord
Can mend the brokenness within me.
Why did he do it?
Yes, he too was broken
And didn't allow You to fix his brokenness.
I can't fix that.

I am calling on You
Right now Lord.
Bind these wounds of betrayal.
Lord, fix me!
Fix me Lord!
Heal me.
My strength is failing.
I call Your name.
Help me Lord!

Different

Not so difficult to understand...

Common held
Beliefs
Values
And
Pain.

Respect for the unique qualities of another!

Outside differences.
Inside visions remain the same.
Different?
Unique?

A puzzle to me.

Discoveries

If I had known that maturity is an
Ongoing journey
Fraught with many planned and unplanned
Experiences.

Inside
I am still young
Vulnerable
Trusting
And
Sexy.

I still have needs.
I am still full of strong
Emotions and
Passions.

Maturity!
Does it ever come?

Or
Does life's lessons
Not cause the same damages as before?

Or
Are we stronger?
Able to adjust to the forces
And power that
The winds of life blow our way?

If I had known that maturity is an
Ongoing process
I would have been
Gentler and
Kinder to
My
Soul.

Do You Care?

Do you care enough to give of yourself?
Do you care enough to truly love?

Is it possible to open up to me?
Do you care enough to risk losing me?

Do you care enough to be in love?

Do We Ever Say Goodbye?

How to say goodbye
Gracefully
Carefully?

I'm circumventing the pain so adroitly
Changing subjects
Dodging issues, evading.

Easing away from goodbye
So much joy
So short a time
Must we say goodbye?

Oh, but we dance so divinely
Skirting the issue of that final, finite, goodbye.

How to say goodbye
When we are gracefully, carefully,
Circumventing the issue so adroitly.

Our lives have merged and become as one.

Do we ever say goodbye?

Or do we just go on?????

Empathy

Each of us has experienced pain
Has worries
Fears and aspirations

Each of us is dealing with issues
Trust issues
Broken promise issues
Self-doubt issues
Anger issues
Issues
Issues

Each of us has felt
Rejection
Pain
Feeling unaccepted

Each of us is human
We need other humans
Our human condition is not singular
It is emotional
Filled with truth
Connected
Peril
Victory
Harshness

Kindness
Forgetfulness
Remember and realize
We are all human beings
We need each other
Empathy

Ever Evolving

Enough already
The day has begun
Ever evolving
Changes
Still changing

I must meet me again
Ever creating
Ever evolving
Changes

Hoping for new beginnings
Facing a new me
Ever evolving
Life changes

Facades

Masks
Facades

Deceits
Facades

Failure to reveal
Facades

No risks
No intimacies
False
Shallow
Losses
Facades

Failure to reveal our inner selves
A high price to pay
To hide

Behind masks
Facades

Deceptions
Facades

No risks
No gains made
Facades

Finding You

To have found you is truly a God given gift
The thoughts that are shared
The love and your care
Your words
Your prayers
And the actions that are shown
To know that I am valued and loved enough
To be utmost in your life
It is a joy
It is the miracle that I have prayed for
To realize that at this age
That love can be so fresh
And as precious as this
I am blessed
We are blessed
It is a blessing to have found you and love again
I am so thankful and happy to share
My life with you
I look forward to our life together
To share your love
To hold you
And to be held by you

First You Laugh And Then You Cry!

After the tears
Then comes the laughter
Fun filled moments
Then pain
And sadness

But then only one
Who is aware
Can laugh at the absurdity
The ridiculousness
The bewildering oceans of oblivion

You laugh and then
You
Cry

Fellow caregivers
Who understand the
Laughter and the
Pain

Only someone who has been there
Is there

Is caring
Is trying to keep our heads
Above water
Treading
Weaving
Laughing to keep from crying
Through the travesty
Through the tapestry of

Caregiving

For Real

Being for real
Authentic
Genuine

So many are not
Smiles hide the
Ugliness beneath the mask

Be for real

It's found in few and far between
Such a quality does exist

For real is an entity itself

Fresh

Excess baggage
Must be jettisoned
Fresh
Vibrant
New Beginnings
Starting over
Trying again
No guarantees
Just blind faith
And new choices

Excess baggage emptied
Jettisoned
Starting fresh
And
Brand new
Fresh

Frustration

Time
A slow, sluggish beast that shows
Allegiance to no man
Power or
Being
Time
Minutes, days, weeks, months, years
Always moving at its own private pace
Time
Time is its own boss
Time bows to no pressure on earth.

Getting To Myself

This journey has many steps
Sidesteps
Boulders
Mountains
And obstacles along our paths

Unexplored
Avenues of greatness
Blocked by self-doubt
And denial

The journey of life
Ebbs and flows
Seasonal tides of great joys
And
Eddies of deep sorrow

Giving Away Me

All of my life
Trained to give
First to parents then to
Husband
Children
Job
Friends

Giving away parts of me
Dreams for me
Giving Away me

Caring for me
Learning finally to give back to me
Loving me
Caring for me
Gathering the pieces of me
And
Regaining myself

Glimmer

I caught a glimmer of greatness today

A glimmer of the once proud, strong,
Brilliant man
I loved
I love

The glimmer took my breath away
It only stayed for a few moments
And I basked in that glow

Then I turned away, only for a moment
And then it was gone

I remembered and cherished that
Glimmer with pure joy
Basking in the memory of what once was our
Reality.

Grateful

I'm grateful for your love
Your trust
Understanding
And your belief in me
I'm grateful for you
And the love that you show
Loving
Silent
Forgiving
And trusting
I'm grateful for your love

Here I Go Again

Here I go again
Do I trust myself to make the right decision?

Can I take the chance of losing
Again?

Here I go again
Trust myself to make the right decision

Do I trust myself
Again?

Or just let go

And let God lead?

Here I go again.

Help me Lord please.

I am in your hands.

If I Had Known

If I had known that you would have gone so
Swiftly
I would have fought harder for us to travel more
Share more
Cuddled and watched more sunsets
Visited more friends
Risked trying more new experiences

If I had known that the time would be shorter
I would have loved you a little more
Hugged a little more
Smiled a little more
Cuddled a little more
Danced in your arms a little more

If I had known then what I know now
We would have talked more
Discovered a little more
And
Reverenced our love just a little more

If I had known
I would have
Held your hand
And kissed you
A little longer

Ignorance of Loss

What I didn't know
How could I know
What I would feel
When I drove away
And left you there?
How could I know the level of pain
That would take me to my knees?
Or that the waves of despair would come in
Unexpected minutes?
Moments of abject PAIN!
Nothing could prepare me
For the raw gut wrenching reality
That you are never coming home.
What I did not know allowed me to survive this
In my heart and head!
I know that it is the right thing to do.
I must do
I need to do
I am compelled to do.
But!
What I did not know was the
Level and depth of my pain!
But,
What I did know is that

It would and will never be easy to
Say goodbye!
Goodbye to my dreams
And hello to this
New reality.

I Want My Own Man at Midnight

Now that my tears have subsided and
My grief is not the jagged raw shards of
Exposed pain
I can stop
Take a breath and remember the joy of having
My own man at midnight.

The pleasure of shared, sacred moments
Reminisces of the sweet savor of satiated,
Satisfying
Soothing, lovemaking memories of
Naked desires
Being desirable, wanton and extremely satisfied.

Stolen moments of joy, touches
And the soothing language of common ground.
In the twilight time
After the sharing and caring of
My life and my love
I want my own man at midnight.

Friends
I know you do care and
Empathize with some of my agony
I know you mean well
But you cannot know the depths of
My pain and sorrow.

It is rewarding to know that you, my friends
Want to assuage my pain and my loss.

But after I leave you or you leave me
After those moments of shared compassion
It is still not the same.

You cannot match what I had
What I felt
What I needed
What I need.

You see
I can share with you
Spend time in your company
Feel your support
Accept your comforting hospitality and
Kind gestures.
The time spent with me, but you see...

I want what I had
What I lost
What I was gifted
What I had on loan from the Lord.

You see
I want my own man at midnight to share
My love
My care
To share me.

Thank you
But no thanks!!!
I want my own man at midnight
To turn to
To lean on
To share my life
To share my love
To love me.

And it is possible
Again
I believe I can have
My own man at midnight.

I Wish You Love

Heartbreaks
Loss
Losses
And
Moments of
Supreme joy
Ecstasy
And
Passion
Is what it looks like
Is what it feels like
Once again and once more
Once again and
One more time
Love is
Unconditional and
Eternal
I wish you love

I Wonder

I wonder if people knew how it
Hurts another life
When they do the things they do

I wonder if they could imagine the pain left
Behind in their reckless pursuit of their own
Selfish needs

It's as though nothing or no one's life is
Important except Their own

I wonder if people ever know the destruction
Left behind
When they do the things they do

In the Moment

Fleeting moments
Scraps of memories
Photo flashes
Insights
Tears
Streaks of greatness
Accomplishments
Failures
Setbacks
Achievements
Passions
Pleasures
Losses
Gains
Joys
Pains
Flashes of insight
Revelations of glory
Rising
Falling
Getting up
Falling down
Getting back up
Floating on
In the moment
Through the vapors of life

Inertia

I wonder how long the
Healing
Learning
Experiencing
Will take

Still struggling
Still revisiting items once conquered

Still wondering
Still solving
Still thinking

Inert
Stuck in emotion
Floating
Suspended motion

Still
After all this time
I am still inert

It Happened!

You said it.
It happened!
I did not imagine it.

It happened!
The sign has been given,
Your love is for real.

It happened!
You said it.

I could never have imagined it would
Come true.
But you said,
"I love you."

And yes, "I do love you, too!"
It happened!

Kindred Spirits

Smiles
Open Conversation
No fear
Opening of hearts
Closing of wounds
Joys
The human condition
Expressed
In the soft stolen moments of life
Kindred Spirits

Longing

Longing for that return to joy
Longing for that return to passionate embraces

Longing
For that undying love in your eyes

Longing
For mingled hearts filled with love once again

Longing
To feel that passion of that first kiss
That first ultimate
Mingling
Longing

Longing
For that passion
That joining
That flame of joy
Basking in your love

Longing
Longing

Still longing

Losing a Friend

How did you know that a close friend is ailing?
How did you know?
When no contact had been made that someone
You loved has been ill and in pain?
How?

The heart knows when its rhythm is broken
It fills the absence of the timeless bond of love.

A friend feels the pain
And the aches that remain
Left behind like ashes
From a once blazing flame.

Friends feel the signals of another in distress.
Words have no need to be spoken.
The heart reigns
Without any boundaries of time.

Lost in Love

The first time I saw you
My stomach fluttered a little
I was surprised at my reaction
It seemed so unreal
I looked at you
We matched glances
Our souls connected in that moment
I smiled and it took your breath away
After that first gaze
We smiled
Butterflies began again
I felt the attraction throughout my body

Our first dance magnificent
Seeing you in awe of me
And I of you
I felt you
Feelings I had forgotten
Began flooding my body
Your moves were sensual and
Stimulating to put it mildly
My heart did a little flip flop
My breathing became difficult
My nostrils flared naturally
Inhaling your wonderful cologne
The smell of you
Lost in lust

Our first delicious kiss
Came with your firm
Strong hands encircling my waist
I felt your strength as
You drew me into your subtle sexiness
Skin black as the night
Smooth as glass
Eyes that reflected my beauty
And your look of adoration
Found in you

The joy and excitement
Waiting to see you
Wanting to be touched
And to touch you
Pure joy
Knowing these feelings were mutual
Being returned and reciprocated
Discovering new found similarities
Enjoying our time
Simplicities and complexities
Together
My joy complete

The sound of your voice
The touch of your hand
The kiss of your lips
Intoxicating me

Surrounding me with your love
Oh yes
It is lovely
We are
Lost in love

Love

Feelings, emotions, and auras transcending time
Space
And places.

Colors
Textures
Places of origin
Have no bearing on
Feelings, emotions or sensations.

Senses respond to positive
Stimuli
Feelings
Emotions.

Love transcends through time.

Love's Goodbye

Learning to say goodbye is the hardest
Thing to do.
Knowing I can still love
And
That love is not enough.
Goodbye my love.

I can survive, forgive and endure to
Love again.

Memories Flood

Memories flood my heart and my mind
Broken melodies
Old pictures
Love notes
Cards of times gone by

Memories flood my heart and my mind
Patches of life appear
Words
Thoughts
Music
Colors
Places in time

Memories flood my heart and my mind
Bittersweet pain remembered
Laughter
Sudden moments of revelations
Memories flood my heart and my mind

My Reality Of Me Without You

At first I was lost
And
Utterly in despair
Then quiet tears and pain took over

Slowly sobs lessened
And memories of joyous
Moments would flood my heart and soul
Full of quiet reflections of
Intimacies shared
In the middle of the night
I basked in us

Waking up in darkness
Expecting to hear you
See you
Touch you
The harsh reality appears
And I am alone
Without you

Oblivion

When does it end?
I know that this is worse for you
Than it is for me
The muddled thinking
The wandering
The madness
The constant asking
Seeking
Looking
Searching for answers
You used to know
Should know
Need to know
Questioning about
Tomorrow
Reassurance needed
Searching for
Acceptance and Love
In this journey into
Oblivion
Will love win
Inspite of the uncertainty
The pain
The loss
And the losses

When it ends
Peace shall come
And
Love will abide
Forever.

Once Again

Once again, I have
Questions
Doubts and
Sad thoughts.

Did I do anything wrong or
Did you get cold feet and change your mind?

What's up with that?

Did you erase the time we spent together?

Did you forget the warm kisses and the
Giving of our
Physical selves to one another?

How do you do that?

Is it better to pretend that it did not exist?
Never happened!

Or do you just breathe
Deeply and clear your mind?

Forget it!

It doesn't happen easily.
Once again, I have questions
Doubts and sad thoughts.

Opening Myself To Love

Fresh
Unfettered love
Risking and
Opening myself to love

Timid and a little leery
Taking a chance and
Opening myself to love

Taking chances
Exploring unfamiliar waters
Discovering unknown territory
I am opening myself to love

New beginnings
A priceless journey
Exhilarating experiences
Unchartered waters
Uninhibited passions
Unbridled joy
Unleased laughter
Joy
Enjoying myself in love

Fresh
Opportunities
Compassion
Tenderness
Caring
Understanding
Heartfelt bliss
Being in love

Pressure

Must I do it now?
Right now?
Why?
Why right now?

Because you said so?
Does this make it so?

Must I do it right now?
Why?

I have some other things to do.
Now, right now?
What about my needs?

Now?
Now, you say.

Do it right now?
Is it an imperative command?
Now?
Okay!
Now?

When will I be free to be
Me?

Questions

Questions of tomorrow
Nearness
Closeness
Uselessness
Questions of tomorrow
Nearness is perceived
As being in the approximate vicinity
They say the earth is near the sun
Is it?
What is true?
Nearness
Closeness remains
Distance reigns
Questions of tomorrow.

Release

Letting go of yesterday
Living for today
Letting go of fear
Looking forward to today
Letting go of sorrow
Shedding silent tears of pain
Letting go of hate
Healing
Beginning
Renewing
Letting go of the known
Reaching toward
The
Future

Rest Now, My Beloved

The Lord giveth and the
Lord taketh away
Blessed be the name of the Lord

Thank you for the love the joy
And the companionship
For the moments lived together and each day
Ruminating in our love

Thank you for the reality and pain
Of loving and caring for each other

Thank you
Lord for the gift of my
Forever and One Day Love

We who loved you will remember
And cherish the essence of who you were
Blessed be the name of the Lord
Who doeth all things well

We praise You Lord
And lift up our loved one to Your
Ever loving and
Everlasting arms

We will see you again
Love you forever and one day
My Beloved
Always

Social Distancing

Another season
Social Distancing
Still in denial
Aching to be held
But no hugs no touching
Behind the masks
To save my outer body

Yet inward
My soul is longing
To blend closely with you

Longing for the norm
But realizing that it will never be

Social distancing does not allow the touch
I so desire
Thankful for love and light
Still here leading
Filling my
Soul with warmth and
Love

Soulmate?

I hope my heart is treasured
With as much value
As
Yours is with me.

I feel your love
And need to verify
Myself with you.

I am blindly without
Restraint
Depending
And
Trusting
You
With
My
Soul.

Still

Still
After all this time
Still

After all this time
Knowledge wasted
Moments lost
Memories escape
Experiences lost
Still

After all this time
Years
Weeks
Opportunities missed
Still

After all these years
Caring is forever
Loving is forever
After all this time
I'm here
Still

Taking A Chance

Oh, I see you looking at me
I am surely looking at you

Hey there, how are you?

I don't mind flirty or flashing
Fresh looks of invitation
The feelings appear to be mutual

I'm good, and you?

Mysterious man with inquisitive eyes
Magnetism
Strong attraction
Raw
Sensual feelings course through me
Stirring
Unknown entity

Oh, I see you!

Wondrous moments of uncertainty
Passion, lust and possibilities

Yes, I am seeing you
Are you feeling me?!

Thank You

Oh how good you made me feel
Your hugs
Your smiles
Your tears
Your kisses
You made me feel
So pure
So blessed
Oh, how good you made me feel
You cleansed
My heart
My soul
My mind
And chased away my fears
Oh how good you made me feel
Sharing your love
Thank you

The Heart

Miles may be far
Yet the heart knows no boundaries

One can go home again

Miles cannot separate the heart as
It knows no boundaries

With no boundaries
The heart will always have a home

The heart has
No limitations
Just like love

Love has
No boundaries
No distances

Love can bind or confine
But
The heart
And
Love
Remain
Eternal

The Journey of Dementia

The sadness and anxiety
Of this thing called
Dementia
The loneliness
Isolation and pain
Moments of remembrance
Brilliance
Then poof
Gone
Vanished
Into the oblivion of
Dementia
Blank expressions
Total confusion
Wait
There it is
A quick flash of a smile
Joy
A warm embrace
No! Oh, no!
Now gone into the
Panic filled madness
Dementia
Loss
Losses
The fading away

Memories forgotten
Unrecognized
Unglued
Unraveling
Fading away of the brilliance
The monster wins!

The Long Goodbye

First, you cry and then you
Wipe the tears
And dry your eyes
Sadness creeps
Into the very marrow of your bones
The pain strikes and
Takes your breath
Away
Then you tear up again
And the memories flood your
Soul
Snatches of joys from
Moments long ago
Remembered passions and
Moments of ecstasy
Then reality hits and you look into
The eyes of your loved one
Who is there but not

A shell of what once was

Yet
You remember
And
Inside
You are saying
A long goodbye
To what will never be, again.

The Poison Of The Tongue

Ugly words are
Like a poison
Slowly spreading through each body it
Encounters
Destroying each cell
Slowly evading the core
And leaving death and destruction behind

Poisonous venom
Lashed out
Coiled and ready to destroy
Twisted
Waiting to attack

Sprung into action by
A simple word or innocent act

Viperous eyes shielded to hide the destruction
Ready to be unleashed
Attack
Strike
Withdraw

Slithering away
Silently watching the destruction
Left behind
Veiled eyes
See the victim paralyzed by the venomous
Words left behind

The victory of a two edged sword
Wounding the
Soul of the victim and its attacker
A deadly snake
Leaving poisonous venom behind
Destroying the soul

The Relentless Nightmare

Such uncertainty.
One moment lucidity,
Normalness.
Next hour, frantic behavior
Defiance and anger.

Next!
Neediness
Cries for affection and warmth.
Then Dr. Jekyll rears his ugly head
Angry outbursts.

Then calmness
Along with gentle interludes of peace.

The storms are brewing.
The demon captures and strips away the mind
And the soul
Of this individual whom I love.
Gradually
And with malice
Until you
Or they
Become strangers in the
Midst of time and shared space.

This nightmare continues and continues.

Please say it's possible to wake up and
This nightmare be over.

Wake up.
The truth?
I am awake.
And it is not a dream
This is a harsh reality.
The bogeyman of Dementia is real.
I cannot stop the destructive path of this
Slow, steady pace of the erasing of memory
And mind.

Love cannot cure it
Or heal it
Or turn it away.
But love
Divine
Love
Will transcend through the darkness
Into the universe of their soul
And touch their heart
At times.

Sometimes.

The Saga Continues

One day at a time is the only way
To address such uncertainty
I rage against the wind
To no avail
The saga continues
Each day we try again

Great success this day
Tomorrow we start
Anew

If only the good days could continue
Then the madness comes
Showing up unexpectedly
When times were so good

The saga continues
Reminding you once again
This decline is ongoing and inevitable
The saga continues holding
Both you and them hostage
In the wake of its descent

The Wedding Union

The union of two
Souls who have made the commitment
To love each other unconditionally.

It is the
You
Joining together in hearts and minds.
It's caring for each other
In good times and bad times.
It is sharing and making oneself vulnerable to
Love and the possibility of
Being hurt, not being understood.
It is trusting someone in addition to the Lord
To love you in spite of
Your weaknesses and human frailties.

Love and sacrifice are synonymous.
One cannot live without the other.

On this day you are making a lifetime
Commitment
To share your life with each other
It is not to be taken lightly, as simply a
Ceremonial procedure.
It is the sharing of your
Souls

Your time, your money, your life, your bodies
Without factoring percentages given by
Either one.
It is a full
All in approach
To life and love.

In order to make the long haul of marriage
Know that this is a lifetime commitment
Headed by
Divine intervention and
Immersion in His Love.
The greatest gift is Love.
Love each other.
Commit to each other every day.
Pray for
Divine guidance daily
And your marriage
And your love will be a blessing for the ages.

Today the Elders both past and present are
Praying for you and for your
Love to
Endure throughout
Eternity.
On this day and forever
May your
Love endure.

Thoughts of the Day

This day is not ours
It is the Lord's.
What did you do with the life he gave?
Did you share your gift?
Or squander it away?
Did you help someone or hurt them?
Did you give a smile?
Have a kind word?
What did you do to make a difference in the
Life of man?
Did you entertain angels, unaware,
Or did you even care?
Man that is born of a woman is of few days
And full of sorrow.
What did you do with the day He gave?
What legacy did you leave this day?

Tired Mother

What's best for me?
I have sacrificed for children

Job
Church
Others

Now, I want to do what's best, just for me.
It's my time
My life
My chance

I want to do what's best, just for me.

I don't want to consider
I don't want to debate
I don't want to do anything right now

Now I just want to do what's best, just for me.

To Kiss You

To love you physically
Mentally
Spiritually
You are my love
And I am so grateful for this opportunity
And for you

Let's make this an eternal celebration of our love
Let's continue to show our love and care
For each other
For our sweet kisses
You are my love

Thank God for this blessing
It is a blessing to have found you and love again

Torn

Angst
Grief
Then
Anger
All the many stages of grief
Manifested itself
Torn between pain
Death
And heartaches
Pain from empty promises
Unfulfilled dreams
Anger
Despair
Lost opportunities
Torn
But in the
Slow process
Of
Healing
Now the work begins
But still
Torn
Tread mill
Learning to adjust to life is like
Living on a treadmill
One can choose to run themselves

To death
In their frantic drive for excellence
Or one can take the time to step-off
Rest and taste the beauty along the way
Contemplate and appreciate the
Beauty of just being alive

Understanding

To understand where you are going
You must examine where they have been
Look upon familiar routes
Change them or reroute the places
And explore new spaces
To understand where you are going
You must first recognize where you have been

What Do You Value?

What makes you value the moment?
The person?
The place or
The time?

What makes you want to never forget?

What makes you want that instant,
That experience,
That feeling to remain fresh,
At the forefront of your thoughts?

Permanently etched in perfection
And time?
Is it the person?
The place?
Or the moment in time?
What makes it valuable to you?

How do you value this moment?
This person?
This time?
This treasure?
What do you treasure?

What Love Really Looks Like!

What I have learned is that
Love is not always pretty, nice or beautiful.
It can be messy.
It can even stink and leave a stench lasting a
Lifetime
Or so it seems.
In love there can be moments of great pain and
Great joy
Extreme loneliness and sorrow.
There are years of caring for
With the appearance of not being appreciated
Or the appearance may actually be the case.
Love can be blind
Or lack the willingness to face the truth
Or truths about one's life.
Love is being there and loving when it is not easy.
Love is being there through the hurt
Through the painful words
Unanswered questions
And unshared dreams.

What love and loving is…
It is unconditional
In spite of the circumstances.
It is showing up one more time
Even when hope has been lost.

It is love for that disrespectful spouse.
It's loving that imperfect being.
Recognize that face in the mirror too!
It is needing to pray
Needing to forgive
To give when it feels there's nothing left…
Love is eternal.
It is loving an imperfect being in spite of
Their warts
Their flaws
And
Their conditions.
It's finding that in and during the process of
Being and doing
The greatest love of all is
Unconditional love!

Strengthened by the unconditional love which
God has instilled in us.
His power inside of us is
The only way one can love unconditionally.
Remembering He showed us this love
When He sacrificed his only Son.
At the cross we find love.

Love is messy, hurtful, bloody, hard and
Painful at times.
But through it all
It is the love that shines through

In all of life's impossible circumstances.
Love and loving are the only reason for
Being on this earth.
Messy, smelly, hurting, hurtful,
And breathtaking in its beauty.

Wow, I Found My Man At Midnight

You see
I found my man

I asked for special direction
I made a list
Put my requests in the Holy book
Prayed over it

God stepped in
Saw my needs and answered my prayers

Helped me recover from my loss

Healed my grief and opened my heart
Gave me the opportunity to love again

He sent this man into my life
Who fulfills me

You see
My heart's desire was to have
My own man at midnight
And my dream is now
My reality

Thank you, Lord!

Acknowledgements

I give all honor and glory to my precious Lord for His gift of Jesus and the gifts that He has given to me. I thank Him for His love, guidance and protection.

To Jo Lena Johnson of the Absolute Good Enterprises Publishing Company for seeing the value of my poetry and your earnest and wholehearted support of my writing. Thank you. And the fact that you are my Soror is just so awesome.

To my parents, Lela and Leonard Hall who've always had faith in me. Thanks for your prayers, guidance, spiritual training, sacrifices and your absolute love for me, and for supporting my educational goals and my children. Also, for teaching me to value and love myself, our culture, and our family.

I am grateful for my church families throughout my life: Mt. Zion Missionary Baptist Church in Springfield, Ohio - the late Pastor Rev. W.E. Richardson, Sr., Shiloh Baptist Church in Dayton, Ohio - the late Pastor H. L. Parker. Mt. Zion Baptist Church in East St. Louis, Illinois- the late Pastor John H Rouse. My present church,

Friendly Temple Missionary Baptist Church in St. Louis, Missouri - Bishop Michael F. Jones, Sr. Each of these church families and pastors nurtured my life through their leadership, guidance and biblical teachings.

I am thankful for being a member of Delta Sigma Theta Sorority, Inc., and to my line sisters of the Dayton Alumnae Chapter, La Grande Premiere Fall 1988, who have supported and encouraged me every step of the way. Special love to Beverly Moody and Rachel Johnston. To the St. Louis Alumnae Chapter, special thanks to the Sorors on the June Luncheon Committee who encouraged me to write a poem dedicated to our sisterhood.

To the Redman Writers Guild under the leadership of Dr. Eugene Redmond who welcomed me at all their events with open arms. I especially thank Darlene Roy, also a Delta Soror, who continued to reach out and encourage me. I thank Joyce McKinney for the introduction.

To my St. Louis Sister Friends who have never stopped believing in me: Jeane, Dorothy, Kimberly, Gloria, Georgia, Kwamina, Ruth, NJ, and Mary.

Thanks to Deborah Bennett Peterson who gave me an opportunity to present my poetry at the African Heritage Gala in 1993, at the Dayton

Art Institute for the DCDC Associates. What a memorable experience! This gave me the desire and courage to publish my poetry. Thanks for your unfailing love and support.

To the Ferguson Writers Group with whom I have been a member for well over a decade, our writing retreats and your creative inspiration have been a blessing. And, to Mrs. Carolyn Herkstroeter whose love and encouragement never wavered in wanting to see me as a published poet. Thank you for the opportunity to give a poetry reading to your chapter of the Association of American University Women.

To my Heavenly Angels whose support kept me writing and gave me inspiration because of your love: MaryAnne Mehaffie, Nancy Cox, Craig Wallace, Vinson Taylor and Deanna Mills. Each of you are missed and hold a piece of my heart.

To my lifelong friend Marva Boswell and my cousin Carol Thompson. There's so much to be said for over 60 years! Thanks for being you.

To my 50 year friends, Elaine Stringer and Carolyn Jackson. You are some of the most loving and caring people on this earth. Thank you.

To Marilyn Williams, my friend and fellow member of the Evermoor's. That poetry convention in Washington D.C. was an invaluable experience. Being with you where we were surrounded by published poets, jump started our forty plus year bond as teachers and writers. Thank you!

To Melba, Wyomina, Flora June, Lisa, Lita and Denise, whose love and support are never ending.

To my spiritual "ride or die" sisters whose prayers of love and support have enabled me to continue healing throughout these many years of rough spots. Marva, Yvonnejannai, Lena, Minnie, Crystal, Jacquelyn, Bernice, Carolyn and Pam. And Stephanie, your prayers along with keeping me close when I needed a friend who understood what losing a spouse entailed were lifesaving.

To my siblings Anthony, Christopher and Karen, sister-cousins Monica, Carol and Andrea, thanks for the love we've shared. To my late sister Gloria and Aunt Elverta, I miss you and love you.

To my late husband Joe Simmons who would have been bursting with pride and love to see me performing and signing my books, thank you, my forever and a day love for your support.

About the Author

Author Teresia Simmons grew up in Springfield, Ohio. She is the second child of Lela and Leonard Hall, the second of five children and the first-born daughter. Her parents were married for sixty-four years before her father passed away in 2011. Shortly after, her family mourned the loss of her younger sister, Gloria.

She earned a B.S. in Education from Eastern Kentucky University and a M.S. in Education with special emphasis in Physical education and Dance from the University of Dayton. She became the first African American employee in the Englewood, Ohio, Northmont City Schools, served as a Physical Education teacher.

She married her first husband, Roy Harper in 1971 and from this union, they adopted two children, Randall and Rabiah. The marriage dissolved in after 12 years. She married Joe Simmons in 2000.

She also taught as an adjunct professor at the University of Dayton and Sinclair Community College. She finished her career at Clayton, retiring after thirty years. After marriage, she settled in St. Louis, Missouri, where she became a certified teacher for the Normandy, Jennings and Ferguson Florissant School Systems.

In 2010, Teresia Simmons began working with a small fitness studio, doing individual coaching and teaching in fitness and weight management until her husband Joe was diagnosed with Dementia and needed full time care. He succumbed to the disease in 2019. During that journey, she found great support while volunteering with the Greater Saint Louis Chapter of the Alzheimer's Association, and is now a trained Volunteer Educator. She has also been actively involved with the Friendly Temple (Church) Alzheimer's Support Group, the only African American focused support group in the area.

At present, she is completely retired and loving it. Teresia is an Advisory Board Member and a 17 year member of the St. Louis Symphony Orchestra InUnison Chorus. She also devotes her time volunteering and serving as a member of Friendly Temple Missionary Baptist Church Health Committee, singing in the choir, and helping with the Repast Committee. She is also a member of the Delta Sigma Theta Sorority, Inc., Saint Louis Alumnae Chapter.

Author Teresia Simmons travels and continues to hone her craft by attending writing and poetry workshops, as she finds great joy in creating works of art based on her vast life experiences, including the joy, pain and commitment of love, sickness and health.